FIX-IT and FORGET-IT®
Healthy
ONE-POT MEALS

75 SUPER EASY SLOW COOKER FAVORITES

HOPE COMERFORD

Photos by Bonnie Matthews

Good Books

New York, New York

Visit our website at www.goodbooks.com.

10 9 8 7 6 5 4 3 2 1

Library of Congress Cataloging-in-Publication Data is available on file.

Cover design by Daniel Brount
Cover photo by Getty Images

Print ISBN: 978-1-68099-473-5
Ebook ISBN: 978-1-68099-477-3

Printed in China

Contents

Welcome to *Fix-It and Forget-It Healthy One-Pot Meals*

Is there anything better than throwing everything into one pot and being able to serve a complete dinner several hours later? No muss. No fuss. No piles of dirty dishes to clean. Just home-cooked food, on your table, all from one pot. *Fix-It and Forget-It Healthy One-Pot Meals* will provide you with homemade, tasty, slow-cooked meals you can feel proud to serve to your family. So, spend less time preparing for and cleaning up from dinner, and more time making some delicious memories at your table.

Few Things You Should Know About Your Slow Cooker . . .

Not all slow cookers are created equal . . . or work equally as well for everyone!

Those of us who use slow cookers frequently know we have our own preferences when it comes to which slow cooker we choose to use. For instance, I love my programmable slow cooker, but there are many programmable slow cookers I've tried that I've strongly disliked. Why? Because some go by increments of 15 or 30 minutes and some go by 4, 6, 8, or 10 hours. I dislike those restrictions, but I have family and friends who don't mind them at all! I am also pretty brand loyal when it comes to my manual slow cookers because I've had great success with those and have had unsuccessful moments with slow cookers of other brands. So, which slow cooker(s) is/are best for your household?

It really depends on how many people you're feeding and if you're gone for long periods of time. Here are my recommendations:

For 2–3 person household	3–5 quart slow cooker
For 4–5 person household	5–6 quart slow cooker
For a 6+ person household	6½–7 quart slow cooker

Large slow cooker advantages/disadvantages:

Advantages:

* You can fit a loaf pan or a baking dish into a 6- or 7-quart, depending on the shape of your cooker. That allows you to make bread or cakes, or even smaller quantities of main dishes. (Take your favorite baking dish and loaf pan along when you shop for a cooker to make sure they'll fit inside.)
* You can feed large groups of people, or make larger quantities of food, allowing for leftovers, or meals, to freeze.

Disadvantages:

* They take up more storage room.
* They don't fit as neatly into a dishwasher.
* If your crock isn't ⅔–¾ full, you may burn your food.

Small slow cooker advantages/disadvantages:

Advantages:

* They're great for lots of appetizers, for serving hot drinks, for baking cakes straight in the crock, and for dorm rooms or apartments.
* Great option for making recipes of smaller quantities.

Disadvantages:
- Food in smaller quantities tends to cook more quickly than larger amounts. So keep an eye on it.
- Chances are, you won't have many leftovers. So, if you like to have leftovers, a smaller slow cooker may not be a good option for you.

My recommendation:

Have at least two slow cookers; one around 3 to 4 quarts and one 6 quarts or larger. A third would be a huge bonus (and a great advantage to your cooking repertoire!). The advantage of having at least a couple is you can make a larger variety of recipes. Also, you can make at least two or three dishes at once for a whole meal.

Manual vs. Programmable

If you are gone for only six to eight hours a day, a manual slow cooker might be just fine for you. If you are gone for more than eight hours during the day, I would highly recommend purchasing a programmable slow cooker that will switch to warm when the cook time you set is up. It will allow you to cook a wider variety of recipes.

The two I use most frequently are my 4-quart manual slow cooker and my 6½-quart programmable slow cooker. I like that I can make smaller portions in my 4-quart slow cooker on days I don't need or want leftovers, but I also love how my 6½-quart slow cooker can accommodate whole chickens, turkey breasts, hams, or big batches of soups. I use them both often.

Get to Know Your Slow Cooker . . .

Plan a little time to get acquainted with your slow cooker. Each slow cooker has its own personality—just like your oven (and your car). Plus, many new slow cookers cook hotter and faster than earlier models. I think that with all of the concern for food safety, the slow-cooker manufacturers have amped up their settings so that "High," "Low," and "Warm" are all higher temperatures than in the older models. That means they cook hotter—and therefore, faster—than the first slow cookers. The beauty of these little machines is that they're supposed to cook low and slow. We count on that when we flip the switch in the morning before we leave the house for ten hours or so. So, because none of us knows what kind of temperament our slow cooker has until we try it out, nor how hot it cooks—don't assume anything. Save yourself a disappointment and make the first recipe in your new slow cooker on a day when you're at home. Cook it for the shortest amount of time the recipe calls for. Then, check the food to see if it's done. Or if you start smelling food that seems to be finished, turn off the cooker and rescue your food.

Also, all slow cookers seem to have a "hot spot," which is of great importance to know, especially when baking with your slow cooker. This spot may tend to burn food in that area if you're not careful. If you're baking directly in your slow cooker, I recommend covering the "hot spot" with some foil.

Tips and Tricks

* Slow cookers tend to work best when they're ⅔ to ¾ of the way full. You may need to increase the cooking time if you've exceeded that amount, or reduce it if you've put in less than that. If you're going to exceed that limit, it would be best to reduce the recipe, or split it between two slow cookers. (Remember how I suggested owning at least two or three slow cookers?)

* Keep your veggies on the bottom. That puts them in more direct contact with the heat. The fuller your slow cooker, the longer it will take its contents to cook. Also, the more densely packed the cooker's contents are, the longer they will take to cook. And finally, the larger the chunks of meat or vegetables, the more time they will need to cook.

- Keep the lid on! Every time you take a peek, you lose 20 minutes of cooking time. Please take this into consideration each time you lift the lid! I know, some of you can't help yourself and are going to lift anyway. Just don't forget to tack on 20 minutes to your cook time for each time you peeked!

- Sometimes it's beneficial to remove the lid. If you'd like your dish to thicken a bit, take the lid off during the last half hour to hour of cooking time.

- If you have a big slow cooker (7- to 8-quart), you can cook a small batch in it by putting the recipe ingredients into an oven-safe baking dish or baking pan and then placing that into the cooker's crock. First, put a trivet or some metal jar rings on the bottom of the crock, and then set your dish or pan on top of them. Or a loaf pan may "hook onto" the top ridges of the crock belonging to a large oval cooker and hang there straight and securely, "baking" a cake or quick bread. Cover the cooker and flip it on.

- The outside of your slow cooker will be hot! Please remember to keep it out of reach of children and keep that in mind for yourself as well!

- Get yourself a quick-read meat thermometer and use it! This helps remove the question of whether or not your meat is fully cooked, and helps prevent you from overcooking your meat as well.

Internal Cooking Temperatures:
- Beef—125–130°F (rare); 140–145°F (medium); 160°F (well-done)
- Pork—140–145°F (rare); 145–150°F (medium); 160°F (well-done)
- Turkey and Chicken—165°F
- Frozen meat: The basic rule of thumb is, don't put frozen meat into the slow cooker. The meat does not reach the proper internal temperature in time. This especially applies to thick cuts of meat! Proceed with caution!

- Add fresh herbs 10 minutes before the end of the cooking time to maximize their flavor.

- If your recipe calls for cooked pasta, add it 10 minutes before the end of the cooking time if the cooker is on High; 30 minutes before the end of the cooking time if it's on Low. Then the pasta won't get mushy.
- If your recipe calls for sour cream or cream, stir it in 5 minutes before the end of the cooking time. You want it to heat but not boil or simmer.

Approximate Slow-Cooker Temperatures (Remember, each slow cooker is different):

- High—212°F–300°F
- Low—170°F–200°F
- Simmer—185°F
- Warm—165°F

Cooked beans freeze well. Store them in freezer bags (squeeze the air out first) or freezer boxes. Cooked and dried bean measurements:

- 16-oz. can, drained = about 1¾ cups beans
- 19-oz. can, drained = about 2 cups beans
- 1 lb. dried beans (about 2½ cups) = 5 cups cooked beans

One-Pot Soups, Stews, Chilies, and Chowders

Black Bean Soup
with Chicken and Salsa

Hope Comerford
Clinton Township, MI

Makes 4–6 servings

Prep. Time: 10 minutes & Cooking Time: 6–8 hours & Ideal slow-cooker size: 5- to 6-qt.

4 cups chicken broth

1 large boneless, skinless
chicken breast

2 (15-oz.) cans black beans,
drained and rinsed

1 (16-oz.) jar salsa

1 cup frozen corn

1 cup sliced fresh mushrooms

½ red onion, chopped

1 jalapeño pepper (whole)

1½ tsp. cumin

Salt, to taste

Pepper, to taste

Toppings

Shredded cheese, *optional*

Sour cream, *optional*

Cilantro, *optional*

Avocado, *optional*

1. Place all ingredients except the toppings in slow cooker. Stir.

2. Cover and cook on Low for 6 to 8 hours.

3. Remove the chicken and shred between 2 forks. Replace back in the soup and stir.

Variation:

You may chop up the jalapeño for extra heat. Leaving it whole provides the flavor without the heat.

Serving suggestion:

Serve garnished with the optional toppings.

Chicken and Corn Soup

Eleanor Larson
Glen Lyon, PA

Makes 4–6 servings
Prep. Time: 15 minutes 🌿 *Cooking Time: 8–9 hours* 🌿 *Ideal slow-cooker size: 4-qt.*

2 whole boneless, skinless
chicken breasts, cubed

1 onion, chopped

1 garlic clove, minced

2 carrots, sliced

2 stalks celery, chopped

2 medium potatoes, cubed

1 tsp. mixed dried herbs

⅓ cup tomato sauce

1 (12-oz.) can cream-style corn

1 (14-oz.) can
whole-kernel corn

3 cups chicken stock

¼ cup chopped Italian parsley

1 tsp. salt

¼ tsp. pepper

1. Combine all ingredients except parsley, salt, and pepper in slow cooker.

2. Cover. Cook on Low for 8 to 9 hours, or until chicken is tender.

3. Add parsley and seasonings 30 minutes before serving

Easy Chicken Tortilla Soup

Becky Harder
Monument, CO

Makes 6–8 servings
Prep. Time: 5–10 minutes ⚬ Cooking Time: 8 hours ⚬ Ideal slow-cooker size: 4- to 5-qt.

4 chicken breast halves

2 (15-oz.)cans black beans, undrained

2 (15-oz.) cans Mexican stewed tomatoes, or Ro*Tel tomatoes

1 cup salsa (mild, medium, or hot, whichever you prefer)

1 (4-oz.) can chopped green chilies

1 (14½-oz.) can tomato sauce

Tortilla chips

1. Combine all ingredients in large slow cooker.

2. Cover. Cook on Low for 8 hours.

3. Just before serving, remove chicken breasts and slice into bite-sized pieces. Stir into soup.

4. Put a handful of tortilla chips in each individual soup bowl. Ladle soup over chips. Top with shredded cheese.

White Chicken Chili

Lucille Hollinger
Richland, PA

Makes 8 servings
Prep. Time: 10 minutes   Cooking Time: 5–6 hours   Ideal slow-cooker size: 3-qt.

4 cups cubed, cooked chicken

2 cups chicken broth

2 (14½-oz.) cans cannellini beans

1 (14½-oz.) can garbanzo beans

1 cup shredded white cheddar cheese

¼ cup chopped onion

¼ cup chopped bell pepper

2 tsp. ground cumin

½ tsp. dried oregano

¼ tsp. cayenne pepper

¼ tsp. salt

1. Combine all ingredients in slow cooker.

2. Cover and cook on Low for 5 to 6 hours.

Tip:

Serve with sour cream, shredded cheese, and tortilla chips.

Variations:

Omit garbanzo beans. Shred chicken instead of cubing it. Add 1 tsp. Italian herb seasoning.
—Beverly Hummel

Good go-alongs with this recipe: Cornbread and salad.

Chicken Barley Chili

Colleen Heatwole
Burton, MI

Makes 10 servings

Prep. Time: 20 minutes   ❦   *Cooking Time: 6–8 hours*   ❦   *Ideal slow-cooker size: 6-qt.*

2 (14½-oz.) cans diced tomatoes

1 (16-oz.) jar salsa

1 cup quick-cooking barley, uncooked

3 cups water

1¾ cups chicken stock

1 (15½-oz.) can black beans, rinsed and drained

3 cups cooked chicken, or turkey, cubed

1 (15¼-oz.) can whole-kernel corn, undrained

1–3 tsp. chili powder, depending on how hot you like your chili

1 tsp. cumin

1 tsp. salt

⅛ tsp. pepper

1. Combine all ingredients in slow cooker.

2. Cover. Cook on Low for 6 to 8 hours, or until barley is tender.

Serving suggestion:
Serve in individual soup bowls topped with sour cream and shredded cheese.

Steak and Wild Rice Soup

Sally Holzem
Schofield, WI

Makes 6 servings
Prep. Time: 15 minutes ⚬ Cooking Time: 5 hours ⚬ Ideal slow-cooker size: 5-qt.

4 cups beef stock

3 cups cubed, cooked roast beef

4 oz. sliced fresh mushrooms

½ cup chopped onion

¼ cup ketchup

2 tsp. cider vinegar

1 tsp. brown sugar

1 tsp. Worcestershire sauce

⅛ tsp. ground mustard

1½ cups cooked wild rice

1 cup frozen peas

1. Combine stock, beef, mushrooms, onion, ketchup, vinegar, brown sugar, Worcestershire sauce, and mustard in slow cooker.

2. Cook on Low for 4 hours.

3. Add rice and peas. Cook an additional hour on Low.

Tip:

Great way to use up scraps of meat and broth left from a roast beef, and a nice way to transform leftover wild rice.

Good go-alongs with this recipe: Crusty rolls and a green salad.

Kale Chowder

Colleen Heatwole
Burton, MI

Makes 8 servings
Prep. Time: 30 minutes ⚘ *Cooking Time: 6 hours* ⚘ *Ideal slow-cooker size: 6-qt.*

8 cups chicken broth

I bunch of kale, cleaned, stems removed, chopped

2 lbs. potatoes, peeled and diced

4 cloves garlic, minced

I medium onion, diced

I lb. cooked ham

½ tsp. pepper, or to taste

1. Combine all ingredients in slow cooker.

2. Cover and cook on Low for 6 hours or until vegetables are tender.

Tip:

If you have "new" potatoes, peeling is optional.

Chipotle Navy Bean Soup

Rebecca Weybright
Manheim, PA

Makes 6 servings
Prep. Time: 10 minutes ⚶ *Cooking Time: 8 hours*
Standing Time: 12 hours ⚶ *Ideal slow-cooker size: 5-qt.*

1½ cups dried navy beans, soaked overnight

1 onion, chopped

1 dried chipotle chili, soaked 10–15 minutes in cold water

4 cups water

1–2 tsp. salt

2 cups canned tomatoes with juice

1. Drain soaked beans.

2. Add to slow cooker with onion, chili, and water.

3. Cover and cook on Low for 8 hours until beans are creamy.

4. Add salt and tomatoes.

5. If desired, use an immersion blender to puree soup.

Beef Vegetable Soup

Anona M. Teel
Bangor, PA

Makes 6 servings

Prep. Time: 15 minutes ⚜ *Cooking Time: 8–10 hours* ⚜ *Ideal slow-cooker size: 6½-qt.*

1–1½-lb. soup bone
1 lb. stewing beef cubes
1½ qts. cold water
1 Tbsp. salt
¾ cup diced celery
¾ cup diced carrots
¾ cup diced potatoes
¾ cup diced onion
1 cup frozen mixed vegetables of your choice
1 (16-oz.) can diced tomatoes
⅛ tsp. pepper
1 Tbsp. chopped dried parsley

1. Put all ingredients in slow cooker.

2. Cover. Cook on Low for 8 to 10 hours. Remove bone before serving.

Minestrone Soup

Dorothy Shank
Sterling, IL

Makes 8 servings

Prep. Time: 10 minutes ⚬ *Cooking Time: 4–12 hours* ⚬ *Ideal slow-cooker size: 4- to 5-qt.*

3 cups beef stock

1½ lbs. stewing meat, cut into bite-sized pieces

1 medium onion, diced

4 carrots, diced

1 (14½-oz. can diced tomatoes

1 tsp. salt

1 (10-oz.) pkg. frozen mixed vegetables, or your choice of frozen vegetables

1 Tbsp. dried basil

½ cup dry elbow noodles, vermicelli, or other pasta

1 tsp. dried oregano

1. Combine all ingredients in slow cooker. Stir well.

2. Cover. Cook on Low for 10 to 12 hours, or on High for 4 to 5 hours.

Serving suggestion:

Top individual servings with grated Parmesan cheese.

Tuscan Beef Stew

Orpha Herr
Andover, NY

Makes 12 servings
Prep. Time: 20 minutes & *Cooking Time: 8–9 hours* & *Ideal slow-cooker size: 6-qt.*

1 (10¾-oz.) can tomato soup

1½ cups beef broth

½ cup burgundy wine or other red wine

1 tsp. Italian herb seasoning

½ tsp. garlic powder

1 (14½-oz.) can diced Italian-style tomatoes, undrained

½ cup diced onion

3 large carrots, cut in 1-inch pieces

2 lbs. stew beef, cut into 1-inch pieces

2 (16-oz.) cans cannellini beans, rinsed and drained

1. Stir soup, broth, wine, Italian seasoning, garlic powder, tomatoes, onion, carrots, and beef into slow cooker.

2. Cover and cook on Low for 8 to 9 hours or until vegetables are tender-crisp.

3. Stir in beans. Turn to High until heated through, 10 to 20 minutes more.

Split Pea Soup

Kelly Amos
Pittsboro, NC

Makes 8 servings

Prep. Time: 10 minutes ⚮ *Cooking Time: 8–9 hours* ⚮ *Ideal slow-cooker size: 4½-qt.*

2 cups dry split peas

8 cups water

2 onions, chopped

2 carrots, peeled and sliced

4 slices Canadian bacon, chopped

2 Tbsp. chicken bouillon granules, or 2 chicken bouillon cubes

1 tsp. salt

¼–½ tsp. pepper

1. Combine all ingredients in slow cooker.

2. Cover. Cook on Low for 8 to 9 hours.

Variation:

For a creamier soup, remove half of the soup when done and puree. Stir back into rest of soup.

Cider and Pork Stew

Veronica Sabo
Shelton, CT

Makes 5 servings
Prep. Time: 15 minutes ⚬ Cooking Time: 7–9 hours ⚬ Ideal slow-cooker size: 3½-qt.

2 medium (about 1¼ lbs.) sweet potatoes, peeled if you wish, and cut into ¾-inch pieces

3 small carrots, peeled and cut into ½-inch-thick slices

1 cup chopped onions

1–2-lb. boneless pork shoulder, cut into 1-inch cubes

1 large Granny Smith apple, peeled, cored, and coarsely chopped

¼ cup flour

¾ tsp. salt

½ tsp. dried sage

½ tsp. thyme

½ tsp. pepper

1 cup apple cider

1. Layer sweet potatoes, carrots, onions, pork, and apple in slow cooker.

2. Combine flour, salt, sage, thyme, and pepper in medium bowl.

3. Add cider to flour and spice mix. Stir until smooth.

4. Pour over meat and vegetables in slow cooker.

5. Cover. Cook on Low for 7 to 9 hours, or until meat and vegetables are tender.

Italian Shredded Pork Stew

Emily Fox
Bernville, PA

Makes: 6–8 servings

Prep. Time: 20 minutes   ❧   Cooking Time: 8 hours   ❧   Ideal slow-cooker size: 5-qt.

2 medium sweet potatoes,
peeled and cubed

2 cups chopped fresh kale

1 large onion, chopped

3 cloves garlic, minced

2½–3½ lb. boneless pork
shoulder butt roast

1 (14-oz.) can white kidney or
cannellini beans, drained

1½ tsp. Italian seasoning

½ tsp. salt

½ tsp. pepper

3 (14½-oz.) cans chicken broth

Sour cream, *optional*

1. Place sweet potatoes, kale, onion, and garlic in slow cooker.

2. Place roast on vegetables.

3. Add beans and seasonings.

4. Pour the broth over the other ingredients.

5. Cover and cook on Low for 8 to 10 hours or until meat is tender.

6. Remove meat. Skim fat from cooking juices if desired. Shred pork with 2 forks and return to cooker. Heat through.

7. Garnish with sour cream if desired.

All-Vegetable Soup

Jean Harris Robinson
Pemberton, NJ

Makes 8–10 servings
Prep. Time: 25 minutes ❧ *Cooking Time: 4–6 hours* ❧ *Ideal slow-cooker size: 4-qt.*

2 Tbsp. olive oil

I large white onion, Vidalia preferred, diced

2 medium carrots, diced

2 cloves garlic, minced

I (20-oz.) pkg. frozen cubed butternut squash, or 4 cups chopped fresh

2 cups finely chopped cabbage

I cup chopped kale, packed

½ tsp. ground allspice

¼ tsp. ground ginger, or I Tbsp. finely grated fresh ginger

4 sprigs fresh thyme, or I tsp. dried thyme

I tsp. salt, or to taste

14-oz. can diced tomatoes with juice

I qt. no-salt vegetable broth

1. Combine all ingredients in cooker.

2. Cook on Low for 4 to 6 hours until veggies are soft.

Tips:

Refrigerate for several days or freeze for later. It is a family pleaser. I like to prep the vegetables the night before. I often use frozen vegetables and sometimes add leftover green beans or broccoli at the last minute before serving.

Good go-alongs with this recipe:
Add a dollop of Greek yogurt to the top of each bowl. Place some hot cooked grains, such as brown rice or quinoa, in soup bowls before ladling in soup.

Fresh Tomato Soup

Rebecca Leichty
Harrisonburg, VA

Makes 6 servings

Prep. Time: 20–25 minutes ⚘ *Cooking Time: 3–4 hours* ⚘ *Ideal slow-cooker size: 3½- or 4-qt.*

5 cups ripe tomatoes, diced (your choice about whether or not to peel them)

1 Tbsp. tomato paste

4 cups salt-free chicken broth

1 carrot, grated

1 onion, minced

1 Tbsp. garlic, minced

1 tsp. dried basil

Pepper, to taste

2 Tbsp. lemon juice

1 bay leaf

1. Combine all ingredients in slow cooker.

2. Cook on Low for 3 to 4 hours. Stir once while cooking.

3. Remove bay leaf before serving.

Red Lentil Soup

Carolyn Spohn
Shawnee, KS

Makes 4–6 servings
Prep. Time: 20 minutes ❧ Cooking Time: 3–4 hours ❧ Ideal slow-cooker size: 5-qt.

¾ cup red lentils
½ cup brown rice, uncooked
4 cups vegetable broth
1 small potato, diced
2 medium carrots, chopped
1 small onion, chopped
2 cloves garlic, chopped
½ tsp. turmeric
¼ tsp. ground cumin
¼ tsp. ground coriander
Salt, to taste
Pepper, to taste
Plain yogurt, for serving

1. Combine all ingredients except plain yogurt in slow cooker.

2. Cover and cook on High for 3 to 4 hours, until vegetables are soft.

3. Puree with immersion blender until smooth.

4. Serve in bowls with a little plain yogurt dolloped on top.

Tip:

Other orange-colored vegetables can be used with or instead of carrots. Red or orange sweet peppers and/or butternut squash are good. This is a very flexible soup, as you can vary the vegetables according to what you have on hand.

Variation:
Sprinkle with chopped cilantro.

Sweet Potato and Ginger Soup

Jenny Kempf
Bedminster, PA

Makes 4 servings
Prep. Time: 15 minutes ⚜ Cooking Time: 7–8 hours ⚜ Ideal slow-cooker size: 6-qt.

I lb. sweet potatoes, peeled and cubed

2 tsp. coconut oil

2 tsp. chopped garlic

2 tsp. peeled, chopped ginger

2 cups gluten-free vegetable stock

I cup coconut milk

Salt, to taste

Pepper, to taste

2 Tbsp. fresh chopped cilantro

3 green onions, chopped

Cashews, chopped, for garnish

1. Place sweet potatoes in slow cooker with coconut oil, garlic, ginger, vegetable stock, coconut milk, salt, and pepper.

2. Cover and cook on Low for 7 to 8 hours, or until potatoes are tender.

3. Add cilantro and green onions.

4. Puree soup with hand blender or in stand blender. Pour into bowls or serving pot.

5. Sprinkle with cashews and serve.

Coconut-Curried Spinach Pea Soup

Allison Martin
Royal Oak, MI

Makes 12 servings

Prep. Time: 45 minutes ⚭ *Cooking Time: 7–8 hours* ⚭ *Ideal slow-cooker size: 5-qt.*

5 cups water

2 tsp. salt

8 garlic cloves, peeled

4 cups diced sweet potatoes, peeled or unpeeled

1 Tbsp. coconut oil

4 cups chopped onions

1½ tsp. ginger

1½ tsp. turmeric

1½ tsp. cumin

1½ tsp. coriander

½ tsp. cinnamon

½ tsp. cardamom

¼–½ tsp. cayenne, according to your taste preference

Black pepper, to taste

1½ Tbsp. lemon juice

3 cups frozen peas

4 cups torn fresh spinach

14-oz. can low-fat coconut milk

1. Combine all ingredients in your crock and mix well.

2. Cover and cook on Low for 7 to 8 hours, or until the potatoes are tender when poked with a fork.

3. Puree soup with an immersion blender or a potato masher until as smooth as you like.

Serving suggestion
Serve with an optional garnish of fresh cilantro and/or a dollop of nonfat plain Greek yogurt on top.

Cream of Broccoli and Mushroom Soup

Leona Miller
Millersburg, OH

Makes 12 servings
Prep. Time: 20 minutes ⚬ *Cooking Time: 3½–8 hours* ⚬ *Ideal slow-cooker size: 5- or 6-qt.*

8 oz. fresh mushrooms, sliced

2 lbs. fresh broccoli, chopped

3 (10¾-oz.) cans cream of broccoli soup

1 pint half-and-half

4 oz. extra-lean smoked ham, chopped

¼ tsp. black pepper

½ tsp. dried thyme leaves, crushed, *optional*

3 bay leaves, *optional*

1. Combine all ingredients in slow cooker.

2. Cook on Low for 4 to 5 hours or on High for 2 to 3 hours.

3. Remove bay leaves before serving, if using.

White Bean and Chicken Chili

Hope Comerford
Clinton Township, MI

Makes 6–8 servings

Prep. Time: 15 minutes ⚜ *Cooking Time: 8–10 hours* ⚜ *Ideal slow-cooker size: 5-qt.*

2 lbs. boneless, skinless chicken, cut into bite-sized chunks

½ cup dry navy beans, soaked overnight, drained, rinsed

½ cup dry great northern beans, soaked overnight, drained, rinsed

½ cup chopped carrots

1½ cups chopped onion

14½-oz. can petite diced tomatoes

10-oz. can diced tomatoes with lime juice and cilantro

5 cloves garlic, minced

1 (6-oz.) can tomato paste

1 Tbsp. cumin

1 Tbsp. chili powder

1 tsp. salt

¼ tsp. pepper

8 tsp. Better Than Bouillon chicken base

8 cups water

1. Place all ingredients into the crock and stir to mix well.

2. Cover and cook on Low for 8 to 10 hours.

Pumpkin Chili

Hope Comerford
Clinton Township, MI

Makes 8 servings
Prep. Time: 10 minutes ⚘ *Cooking Time: 7–8 hours* ⚘ *Ideal slow-cooker size: 6-qt.*

I (16-oz.) can kidney beans, drained and rinsed

I (16-oz.) can black beans, drained and rinsed

I large onion, chopped

½ green pepper, chopped

I lb. ground turkey

I (15-oz.) can pumpkin puree

4 cups fresh chopped tomatoes

3 Tbsp. garlic powder

I Tbsp. ancho chili powder

I tsp. salt

2 tsp. cumin

¼ tsp. pepper

4 Tbsp. gluten-free beef bouillon granules

5 cups water

1. Place the kidney beans, black beans, onion, and pepper in the crock.

2. Crumble the ground turkey over the top and spoon the pumpkin puree on top of that.

3. Add in the remaining ingredients and stir.

4. Cover and cook on Low for 7 to 8 hours.

Serving suggestion:
Garnish with pumpkin seeds.

Summer Chili

Hope Comerford
Clinton Township, MI

Makes 6 servings
Prep. Time: 15 minutes ⚬ *Cooking Time: 3½–4 hours* ⚬ *Ideal slow-cooker size: 3-qt.*

1 (28-oz.) can Red Gold sliced
tomatoes and zucchini

1 (15-oz.) can tomato sauce

1 (14-oz.) can petite diced
tomatoes with green chilies

1 (15½-oz.) can chili beans

1 (15¼-oz.) can black beans,
drained, rinsed

1 medium onion, roughly
chopped

3 smallish yellow squash,
halved, quartered, and chopped

3 Tbsp. garlic powder

2 Tbsp. onion powder

1 tsp. salt

⅛ tsp. pepper

2 cups water

1. Place all ingredients into the crock and stir.

2. Cover and cook on Low for 3½ to 4 hours.

Creamy Pumpkin Soup

Janeen Troyer
Fairview, MI

Makes 6 servings
Prep. Time: 10 minutes ⚬ *Cooking Time: 2½ hours* ⚬ *Ideal slow-cooker size: 4-qt.*

1 (29-oz.) can pumpkin

2 (15-oz.) cans chicken broth

⅛ tsp. ground nutmeg

¼ tsp. ground allspice

½ tsp. curry powder

⅛ tsp. ground ginger

1 cup cream, at room temperature

1. In slow cooker, mix pumpkin, broth, and spices.

2. Cover and cook on High for 1½ hours and then turn to Low for 1 hour.

3. Add cream 20 minutes before serving.

Sweet Potato Lentil Soup

Joleen Albrecht
Gladstone, MI

Makes 6 servings

Prep. Time: 10–15 minutes ⚬ *Cooking Time: 6 hours* ⚬ *Ideal slow-cooker size: 4-qt.*

4 cups vegetable broth

3 cups (about 1¼ lbs.) peeled and cubed sweet potatoes,

3 medium carrots, chopped

1 medium onion, chopped

4 cloves garlic, minced

1 cup dried lentils, rinsed

½ tsp. ground cumin

¼ tsp. salt

¼ tsp. cayenne pepper

¼ tsp. ground ginger

¼ cup minced fresh cilantro or 1–2 Tbsp. dried cilantro

1. Combine all ingredients in slow cooker.

2. Cover. Cook on Low for 6 hours, or until vegetables are done to your liking.

Black Bean Chili

Joyce Cox
Port Angeles, WA

Makes 8 servings

Prep. Time: 20 minutes ⚘ *Cooking Time: 6–8 hours* ⚘ *Ideal slow-cooker size: 6-qt.*

1½ cups fresh-brewed coffee

1½ cups vegetable broth

2 (15-oz.) cans diced tomatoes with juice

1 (15-oz.) can tomato sauce

8 cups cooked black beans, drained

1 medium yellow onion, diced

4 cloves garlic, minced

2 Tbsp. brown sugar, packed

2 Tbsp. chili powder

1 Tbsp. ground cumin

Salt, to taste

1. Combine all ingredients except salt in slow cooker.

2. Cover and cook on Low for 6 to 8 hours. Add salt near end of cooking.

Tip:

Great served in bowls with cilantro, cubed avocados, Greek yogurt or sour cream, and grated cheese on top.

Variation:

Use 4 15-oz. cans of black beans, rinsed and drained, instead of the 8 cups cooked black beans. Mash some of the beans with a potato masher before adding to cooker. The chili will be thicker.

Chicken and Turkey One-Pot Meals

Creamy Chicken Rice Casserole

Wanda Roth
Napoleon, OH

Makes 8 servings
Prep. Time: 20 minutes ⚭ Cooking Time: 2–6 hours ⚭ Ideal slow-cooker size: 6-qt.

1 cup long-grain rice, uncooked

3 cups water

2 tsp. low-sodium chicken bouillon granules

1 (10¾-oz.) can cream of chicken soup

2 cups chopped, cooked chicken breast

¼ tsp. garlic powder

1 tsp. onion salt

1 cup grated cheddar cheese

1 (16-oz.) bag frozen broccoli, thawed

1. Combine all ingredients except broccoli in slow cooker.

2. Cook on High for 2 to 3 hours or on Low for 4 to 6 hours.

3. One hour before end of cooking time, stir in broccoli.

Chicken and Dumplings

Annabelle Unternahrer
Shipshewana, IN

Makes 5–6 servings

Prep. Time: 25 minutes ⚬ *Cooking Time: 2½–3½ hours* ⚬ *Ideal slow-cooker size: 3- or 4-qt.*

1 lb. uncooked boneless, skinless chicken breasts, cut in 1-inch cubes

1 lb. frozen vegetables of your choice

1 medium onion, diced

3 cups chicken broth, *divided*

1½ cups low-fat buttermilk biscuit mix

1. Combine chicken, vegetables, onion, and chicken broth (reserve ½ cup, plus 1 Tbsp., broth) in slow cooker.

2. Cover. Cook on High for 2 to 3 hours.

3. Mix biscuit mix with reserved broth until moistened. Drop by tablespoonfuls over hot chicken and vegetables.

4. Cover. Cook on High for 10 minutes.

5. Uncover. Cook on High for 20 minutes more.

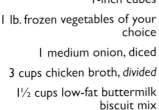

Chicken and Biscuits

Hope Comerford, Clinton Township, MI

Makes 4–6 servings

Prep. Time: 5 minutes & Cooking Time: 6 hours & Ideal slow-cooker size: 3-qt.

2 lbs. boneless, skinless chicken breasts

1 (10½-oz.) can condensed cream of chicken soup

1 (10½-oz.) can condensed cream of potato soup

¾ cup milk

½ tsp. salt

⅛ tsp. pepper

2 tsp. garlic powder

2 tsp. onion powder

1 cup frozen mixed vegetables

6 refrigerator biscuits, cooked according to the package directions

1. Place the chicken in the crock.

2. In a bowl, mix together the cream of chicken soup, cream of potato soup, milk, salt, pepper, garlic powder, onion powder, and frozen mixed vegetables. Pour this over the chicken.

3. Cover and cook on Low for 6 hours.

4. Shred the chicken between two forks and stir back through the contents of the crock.

5. Serve the chicken mixture over the biscuits to serve.

Chicken and Egg Noodle Dinner

Janie Steele
Moore, OK

Makes 5–7 servings
Prep. Time: 15 minutes ⚬ *Cooking Time: 5–6 hours* ⚬ *Ideal slow-cooker size: 5-qt.*

1 lb. chicken breasts

1 can low-sodium cream of chicken soup

2 (15½-oz.) cans low-sodium chicken broth

1 tsp. garlic powder

1 tsp. onion powder

¼ tsp. celery seed

¼ tsp. pepper

4 Tbsp. butter or margarine

1 (24-oz.) bag frozen egg noodles

1. Place chicken in crock with all ingredients except the noodles.

2. Cover and cook for 5 to 6 hours on Low.

3. Remove chicken and shred. Return to slow cooker, then add frozen noodles and cook for an additional 40 to 60 minutes, or until noodles are tender.

Lemon Pepper Chicken with Veggies

Nadine Martinitz, Salina KS
Makes 4 servings

Prep Time: 20 minutes ❧ Cooking Time: 4–10 hours ❧ Ideal slow-cooker size: 4-qt.

4 carrots, sliced ½-inch thick

4 potatoes, cut in 1-inch chunks

2 cloves garlic, peeled and minced, *optional*

4 whole chicken legs and thighs, skin removed

2 tsp. lemon pepper seasoning

1¾ cup low-sodium, gluten-free chicken broth

1. Layer vegetables and chicken in slow cooker.

2. Sprinkle with lemon pepper seasoning and poultry seasoning if you wish. Pour broth over all.

3. Cover and cook on Low for 8 to 10 hours or on High for 4 to 5 hours.

Variation:

Add 2 cups frozen green beans to the bottom layer in the cooker.

—Earnest Zimmerman, Mechanicsburg, PA

Chicken Curry with Rice

Jennifer Yoder Sommers, Harrisonburg, VA

Makes 6 servings
Prep Time: 10 minutes ♣ *Cooking Time: 5–10 hours* ♣ *Ideal slow-cooker size: 3- to 4-qt.*

1½ lbs. boneless, skinless chicken thighs, quartered

1 onion, chopped

2 cups uncooked long-grain rice

2 Tbsp. curry powder

1¾ cups gluten-free, low-sodium chicken broth

1. Combine all ingredients in slow cooker.

2. Cover and cook on Low for 8 to 10 hours, or on High 5 for hours, or until chicken is tender but not dry.

Variation:

Add 1 chopped apple. Thirty minutes before the end of the cooking time, stir in 2 cups frozen peas.

Slow-Cooker Chicken and Salsa

Marcia S. Myer
Manheim, PA

Makes 6 servings

Prep. Time: 10 minutes ⚶ *Cooking Time: 4–10 hours* ⚶ *Ideal slow-cooker size: 5-qt.*

2 (15-oz.) cans black beans

1½ lbs. boneless chicken breasts, cut into serving-size pieces

1 (16-oz.) jar black bean salsa

1 (16-oz.) jar corn salsa

1 cup uncooked brown rice

2 cups water

1 cup sour cream

1 cup shredded cheddar cheese or Mexican blend cheese

1 avocado, sliced, for garnish

Corn chips, for garnish

1. Combine the beans, chicken, black bean salsa, corn salsa, brown rice, and 2 cups water in slow cooker.

2. Cook on High for 4 hours or on Low for 8 to 10 hours, adding water if needed near the end of the cooking time.

3. To serve, place 1½ cups of the chicken mixture on individual serving plates. Top with the sour cream and cheese. Garnish with the avocado and corn chips.

Chicken Cacciatore

Dawn Day
Westminster, CA

Makes 10 servings
Prep. Time: 20 minutes ⚙ *Cooking Time: 5–6 hours* ⚙ *Ideal slow-cooker size: 3-qt.*

2 lbs. uncooked boneless, skinless chicken breasts, cubed

½ lb. fresh mushrooms

1 bell pepper, chopped

1 medium onion, chopped

1 (12-oz.) can chopped tomatoes

1 (6-oz.) can tomato paste

1 (12-oz.) can tomato sauce

½ tsp. dried oregano

½ tsp. dried basil

½ tsp. garlic powder

½ tsp. salt

½ tsp. black pepper

1. Combine all ingredients in slow cooker.

2. Cover. Cook on Low for 5 to 6 hours.

Bacon-Feta Stuffed Chicken

Tina Goss
Duenweg, MO

Makes 4 servings
Prep. Time: 10 minutes & *Cooking Time: 1½–3 hours* & *Ideal slow-cooker size: 3-qt.*

¼ cup crumbled cooked bacon

¼ cup crumbled feta cheese

4 boneless, skinless chicken breast halves

2 (14½-oz.) cans diced tomatoes

1 Tbsp. dried basil

1. In a small bowl, mix bacon and cheese together lightly.

2. Cut a pocket in the thicker side of each chicken breast. Fill each with ¼ of the bacon and cheese. Pinch shut and secure with toothpicks.

3. Place chicken in slow cooker. Top with tomatoes and sprinkle with basil.

4. Cover and cook on High for 1½ to 3 hours, or until chicken is tender, but not dry or mushy.

Apricot Stuffing and Chicken

Elizabeth Colucci
Lancaster, PA

Makes 5 servings
Prep. Time: 10 minutes ❧ *Cooking Time: 2–3½ hours* ❧ *Ideal slow-cooker size: 5-qt.*

I stick (**8 Tbsp.**) butter, *divided*

I box cornbread stuffing mix

4 boneless, skinless chicken breast halves

I (6–8-oz.) jar apricot preserves

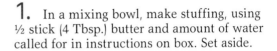

1. In a mixing bowl, make stuffing, using ½ stick (4 Tbsp.) butter and amount of water called for in instructions on box. Set aside.

2. Cut up chicken into 1-inch pieces. Place on bottom of slow cooker. Spoon stuffing over top.

3. In microwave, or on stovetop, melt remaining ½ stick (4 Tbsp.) butter with preserves. Pour over stuffing.

4. Cover and cook on High for 2 hours, or on Low for 3½ hours, or until chicken is tender but not dry.

Roast Chicken or Hen with Veggies

Betty Drescher
Quakertown, PA

Makes 6 servings
Prep. Time: 30 minutes ⚜ Cooking Time: 9–11 hours ⚜ Ideal slow-cooker size: 4- to 5-qt.

2 medium carrots, cut in 1-inch chunks

1 medium onion, cut in wedges

3 medium potatoes, cut in 1-inch chunks

3–4-lb. roasting chicken, or hen

1½ tsp. salt

¼ tsp. pepper

1 tsp. parsley flakes, *divided*

1 Tbsp. butter

½–1 cup water

1. Place carrots, onion, and potatoes in bottom of crock.

2. Thoroughly wash chicken and pat dry. Sprinkle cavity with salt, pepper, and ½ tsp. parsley flakes. Place in slow cooker on top of veggies, breast-side up.

3. Dot with butter or brush with melted butter.

4. Sprinkle with remaining parsley flakes. Add water around the chicken.

5. Cover and cook on High for 1 hour. Turn to Low and cook for 8 to 10 hours.

Tip:

Sprinkle with basil or tarragon in step 4, if you wish.

Simple Lemon Garlic Chicken with Potatoes

Genelle Taylor
Perrysburg, OH

Makes 4–6 servings
Prep. Time: 10 minutes ⚘ Cooking Time: 5–6 hours ⚘ Ideal slow-cooker size: 5- or 6-qt.

4–6 chicken breasts

2 medium potatoes, cubed

2 tsp. minced garlic

¼ cup olive oil

1 Tbsp. parsley flakes

2 Tbsp. lemon juice (or juice of 1 whole lemon)

1. Place chicken breasts and potatoes in slow cooker.

2. Combine garlic, olive oil, parsley flakes, and lemon juice; pour over chicken.

3. Cover and cook on Low for 5 to 6 hours.

Maple-Glazed Turkey Breast with Rice

Jeanette Oberholtzer

Manheim, PA
Makes 4 servings

Prep. Time: 10–15 minutes   ⚬   *Cooking Time: 4–6 hours*   ⚬   *Ideal slow-cooker size: 3- to 4-qt.*

1 (6-oz.) pkg. long-grain wild rice mix

1½ cups water

2-lb. boneless turkey breast, cut into 1½–2-inch chunks

¼ cup maple syrup

1 onion, chopped

¼ tsp. ground cinnamon

½ tsp. salt, *optional*

1. Combine all ingredients in slow cooker.

2. Cook on Low for 4 to 6 hours, or until turkey and rice are both tender, but not dry or mushy.

Turkey "Spaghetti" Quinoa

Hope Comerford
Clinton Township, MI

Makes 8–10 servings

Prep. Time: 10–15 minutes ⚶ *Cooking Time: 5 hours* ⚶ *Ideal slow-cooker size: 5- or 6-qt.*

2 lbs. lean ground turkey

½ tsp. salt

⅛ tsp. pepper

1 tsp. garlic powder

1 tsp. onion powder

1 cup quinoa

1 cup chopped onion

1 cup shredded mozzarella cheese (for dairy-free, replace with dairy-free cheese or leave out)

4 cups tomato sauce

2 cups water

1. Spray crock with nonstick spray.

2. Place all ingredients in crock and stir so everything is mixed.

3. Cover and cook on Low for 5 hours.

"Hash Brown" Cauliflower Breakfast Bake

Hope Comerford
Clinton Township, MI

Makes 8–10 servings
Prep. Time: 20 minutes ⚬ Cooking Time: 7 hours ⚬ Ideal slow-cooker size: 6-qt.

12 eggs

½ cup unsweetened almond milk or milk

1 tsp. kosher salt

1 tsp. garlic powder

1 tsp. onion powder

¼ tsp. pepper

1 head cauliflower, shredded

1 medium onion, chopped

1 lb. turkey sausage, browned and drained

2 cups shredded cheddar cheese, *divided*

1. In a bowl, mix together the eggs, milk, salt, garlic powder, onion powder, and pepper.

2. Spray crock with nonstick spray.

3. Combine the cauliflower, onion, and turkey sausage in a bowl.

4. Spread ⅓ of the cauliflower mix into the bottom of the crock. Top this with ⅓ of the egg mixture, then top with ⅓ of the cheese. Repeat this process 2 more times.

5. Cover and cook on Low for 7 hours.

Cheesy Stuffed Peppers

Jean Moore
Pendleton, IN

Makes 8 servings

Prep. Time: 40 minutes 🍴 *Cooking Time: 3–9 hours*
Ideal slow-cooker size: 4- or 6-qt. (large enough so that all peppers sit on the bottom of the cooker)

8 small green bell peppers, tops removed and seeded

1 (10-oz.) pkg. frozen corn

¾ lb. lean ground turkey

¾ lb. extra-lean ground beef

1 (8-oz.) can tomato sauce

½ tsp. garlic powder

¼ tsp. black pepper

1 cup shredded cheddar cheese

½ tsp. Worcestershire sauce

¼ cup chopped onions

3 Tbsp. water

2 Tbsp. ketchup

1. Wash peppers and drain well. Combine all other ingredients except water and ketchup in mixing bowl. Stir well.

2. Stuff peppers ⅔ full with ground meat mixture.

3. Pour water in slow cooker. Arrange peppers on top.

4. Pour ketchup over peppers.

5. Cover. Cook on High for 3 to 4 hours or on Low for 7 to 9 hours.

Beef and Pork
One-Pot Meals

Red Wine Apple Roast

Rose Hankins
Stevensville, MD

Makes 10 servings

Prep. Time: 15 minutes ⚬ *Cooking Time: 6–8 hours* ⚬ *Ideal slow-cooker size: 4- or 5-qt.*

3-lb. eye of round beef roast

3 cups thinly sliced onions

1½ cups chopped apples, peeled or unpeeled

3 cloves garlic, chopped

I cup red wine

Salt, to taste

Pepper, to taste

1. Put roast in slow cooker. Layer onions, apples, and garlic on top of roast.

2. Carefully pour wine over roast without disturbing its toppings.

3. Sprinkle with salt and pepper to taste.

4. Cover. Cook on Low for 6 to 8 hours, or until meat is tender but not dry.

Texas Pot Roast

Genelle Taylor
Perrysburg, OH

Makes 6 servings
Prep. Time: 15 minutes   ❧   Cooking Time: 8–10 hours   ❧   Ideal slow-cooker size: 6-qt.

2–2½ lb. chuck roast

½ onion, chopped

½ bell pepper (any color), chopped

2 stalks celery, chopped

2 large potatoes, chopped into chunks, *optional*

2 cloves garlic, minced

½ cup tomato sauce

½ cup barbecue sauce

2 beef bouillon cubes

½ cup water

I tsp. salt

I tsp. black pepper

½ tsp. dried thyme

1. Place roast in slow cooker.

2. Top with vegetables. Add potatoes (optional).

3. In small bowl, stir together tomato sauce, barbecue sauce, bouillon cubes, water, and spices. Pour over roast and vegetables.

4. Cook on Low for 8 to 10 hours.

Pot Roast with Carrots and Potatoes

Loretta Hanson, Hendricks, MN
Makes 6 servings

Prep Time: 30 minutes ⚜ Cooking Time: 4–12 hours ⚜ Ideal slow-cooker size: 5- to 6-qt.

3–4 potatoes, peeled and thinly sliced

3–4 carrots, peeled and thinly sliced

1 onion, chopped, *optional*

Salt, to taste

Pepper, to taste

3-lb. brisket, rump roast, or pot roast

1 cup low-sodium, gluten-free beef stock

1. Place vegetables in bottom of slow cooker.

2. Sprinkle meat with salt and pepper to taste. Place meat in the slow cooker.

3. Pour beef stock around meat.

4. Cover and cook on Low for 10 to 12 hours, or on High for 4 to 5 hours.

Uncle Tim's Pot Roast

Tim Smith, Rutledge, PA

Makes 4 servings

Prep Time: 30 minutes & *Cooking Time: 8 hours* & *Ideal slow-cooker size: 5-qt.*

4-lb. eye roast of beef

2 Tbsp. crushed garlic

8 medium red potatoes, halved or quartered

I lb. baby carrots, peeled

Water

I green pepper, cut in half and deseeded

1. Place roast in center of slow cooker. Rub garlic into roast.

2. Add potatoes and carrots. Add water until carrots and potatoes are covered.

3. Cover and cook on Low for 8 hours.

4. One hour before serving, place pepper halves on top of meat (moving vegetables aside as much as possible), cut-side down. Cover and continue cooking.

Variation:

Sprinkle roast with salt and pepper in step 1. And sprinkle potatoes and carrots with salt in step 2.

Slow-Cooker Swiss Steak

Joyce Bowman, Lady Lake, FL

Makes 4 servings

Prep Time: 30 minutes ⚭ *Cooking Time: 7 hours* ⚭ *Ideal slow-cooker size: 3-qt.*

1-lb. round steak, ¾–1-inch thick, cubed

1 (16-oz.) can low-sodium stewed tomatoes

3 carrots, halved lengthwise

2 potatoes, quartered

1 medium onion, quartered

Garlic powder, to taste, *optional*

1. Add all ingredients to slow cooker in the order they are listed.

2. Cover and cook on Low for 7 hours, or until meat and vegetables are tender, but not overcooked or dry.

Corned Beef and Cabbage

Carrie Darby, Wayland, IA
Leona Yoder, Hartville, OH
Esther Porter, Minneapolis, MN
Betty K. Drescher, Quakertown, PA
Karen Ceneviva, New Haven, CT
Bonita Ensenberger, Albuquerque, NM
Dorothy Lingerfelt, Stonyford, CA

Makes 6 servings
Prep Time: 30 minutes ⚬ Cooking Time: 4–7 hours ⚬ Ideal slow-cooker size: 5- or 6-qt.

3–4-lb. corned beef brisket (not in a brine), cut into 6–8 pieces

¾–1¼ cups water

5–6 carrots, cut in 2–3-inch pieces

3 medium onions, quartered

Salt

Pepper

Half to a whole head of cabbage, cut into wedges

1. Place corned beef in slow cooker. Add water.

2. Place carrots and onions around the meat if possible, pushing the vegetables in so they're at least partly covered by the water. Sprinkle salt and pepper over all.

3. Cover and cook on Low for 4 to 5 hours, or on High for 2½ to 3 hours.

4. Add cabbage to cooker, pushing down into liquid to moisten. Turn to High and cook an additional 1½ to 2 hours, or until vegetables and meat are tender but not overcooked.

Variation:

Add 3 medium potatoes, peeled or unpeeled, cut into chunks, to step 2.

—Sharon Timpe, Jackson, WI

Beef with Broccoli

Genelle Taylor
Perrysburg, OH

Makes 4 servings

Prep. Time: 10 minutes ☙ *Cooking Time: 5–6 hours* ☙ *Ideal slow-cooker size: 5- or 6-qt.*

1 cup beef broth

½ cup low-sodium soy sauce

⅓ cup brown sugar

1 Tbsp. sesame oil

3 cloves garlic, minced

1½ lb. boneless beef chuck roast or steak, sliced into thin strips

2 Tbsp. cornstarch

1 (14-oz.) bag frozen broccoli florets

1. In a mixing bowl, whisk together the beef broth, soy sauce, brown sugar, sesame oil, and garlic.

2. Lay the beef strips in slow cooker and pour the sauce over, tossing the strips to coat.

3. Cover and cook on Low for 5 to 6 hours

4. Remove 4 Tbsp. of the sauce and whisk it in a small bowl with cornstarch. Slowly stir this into slow cooker.

5. Add broccoli. Cook an additional 30 minutes.

Low-Fat Slow-Cooker Roast

Charlotte Shaffer
East Earl, PA

Makes 10 servings
Prep. Time: 15 minutes ⚘ *Cooking Time: 3–8 hours* ⚘ *Ideal slow-cooker size: 6-qt.*

3 lb. boneless beef roast

4 carrots, peeled and cut into 2-inch pieces

4 potatoes, cut into quarters

2 onions, quartered

1 cup gluten-free, low-sodium beef broth or stock

1 tsp. garlic powder

1 tsp. Mrs. Dash seasoning

½ tsp. salt

½ tsp. black pepper

1. Place roast in slow cooker.

2. Add carrots around edges, pushing them down so they reach the bottom of the crock.

3. Add potatoes and onions.

4. Mix together broth and seasonings and pour over roast.

5. Cover and cook on Low for 6 to 8 hours, or on High for 3 to 4 hours.

Mexicali Round Steak

Marcia S. Myer
Manheim, PA

Makes 6 servings
Prep. Time: 20 minutes & Cooking Time: 5–6 hours & Ideal slow-cooker size: 5-qt.

1½ lbs. round steak

1 cup frozen corn, thawed

½–1 cup chopped fresh cilantro, according to your taste preference

½ cup beef broth

3 stalks celery, sliced

1 large onion, sliced

1 (20-oz.) jar salsa

1 (15-oz.) can black beans or pinto beans, rinsed and drained

1 cup grated cheddar cheese

1. Cut beef into 6 pieces. Place in slow cooker.

2. Combine remaining ingredients except cheese, and pour over beef.

3. Cover. Cook on Low for 5 to 6 hours.

4. Sprinkle with cheese before serving.

Steak and Rice Dinner

Susan Scheel
West Fargo, ND

Makes 8 servings
Prep. Time: 15–20 minutes & *Cooking Time: 4–6 hours* & *Ideal slow-cooker size: 5-qt.*

I cup uncooked wild rice, rinsed and drained

I cup chopped celery

I cup chopped carrots

2 (4-oz.) cans mushrooms, drained

I large onion, chopped

½ cup slivered almonds

3 beef bouillon cubes

2½ tsp. seasoned salt

2 lbs. boneless round steak, cut in bite-sized pieces

3 cups water

1. Layer ingredients in slow cooker in order listed. Do not stir.

2. Cover. Cook on Low for 4 to 6 hours.

3. Stir before serving.

Easy Sweet-and-Sour Pork Chops

Jeanne Hertzog
Bethlehem, PA

Makes 6 servings
Prep. Time: 5 minutes ⚭ Cooking Time: 7–8 hours ⚭ Ideal slow-cooker size: 4-qt.

1 (16-oz.) bag frozen stir-fry vegetables

6 bone-in pork chops

1 (12-oz.) bottle sweet-and-sour sauce

½ cup water

1 cup frozen pea pods

1. Place stir-fry vegetables in slow cooker. Arrange chops on top.

2. Combine sauce and water. Pour over chops.

3. Cover. Cook on Low for 7 to 8 hours.

4. Turn to High and add pea pods.

5. Cover. Cook on High for 5 minutes.

Applesauce Pork Chops with Sweet Potatoes

Hope Comerford
Clinton Township, MI

Makes 4 servings
Prep. Time: 5 minutes ⚜ *Cooking Time: 7 hours* ⚜ *Ideal slow-cooker size: 4-qt.*

2 lbs. thick cut, bone-in pork chops

3 medium sweet potatoes, cut in 1-inch cubes

1½ cups natural applesauce

¼ cup brown sugar

1–2 Tbsp. minced onion

1 tsp. salt

¼ tsp. pepper

1. Place pork chops and sweet potatoes in crock.

2. In a bowl, mix together the remaining ingredients. Pour this over the pork chops.

3. Cover and cook on Low for 7 hours.

Pork and Sweet Potatoes

Vera F. Schmucker, Goshen, IN

Makes 4 servings
Prep Time: 15 minutes ⚶ *Cooking Time: 4–4½ hours* ⚶ *Ideal slow-cooker size: 4-qt.*

4 pork loin chops

Salt, to taste

Pepper, to taste

4 sweet potatoes, cut in large chunks

2 onions, cut in quarters

½ cup apple cider

1. Place meat in bottom of slow cooker. Salt and pepper to taste.

2. Arrange sweet potatoes and onions over the pork.

3. Pour apple cider over all.

4. Cook on High for 30 minutes and then on Low for 3½ to 4 hours, or until meat and vegetables are tender but not dry.

Cranberry Jalapeño Pork Roast

Hope Comerford
Clinton Township, MI

Makes 4–6 servings

Prep. Time: 10 minutes ⚘ *Cooking Time: 7–8 hours* ⚘ *Ideal slow-cooker size: 3-qt.*

2–3-lb. pork roast

3 medium potatoes, cut in 1-inch chunks

1 tsp. garlic powder

½ tsp. salt

½ tsp. pepper

1 small onion, chopped

½ jalapeño, seeded and diced

1 (14-oz.) can jellied cranberry sauce

1. Place pork roast and potatoes in crock.

2. Season with the garlic powder, salt, and pepper.

3. Dump in the onion and jalapeño.

4. Spoon the jellied cranberry sauce over the top of the contents of the crock.

5. Cover and cook on Low for 7 to 8 hours.

Sausage and Dumplings

MarJanita Geigley
Lancaster, PA

Makes 6 servings

Prep. Time: 30 minutes ⚮ Cooking Time: 4 hours ⚮ Ideal slow-cooker size: 5-qt.

½ large onion, chopped

1½ tsp. butter

4 cups chopped cooked sausage

1 (10¾-oz.) can cream of mushroom soup

1 cup sour cream

½ cup milk

½ cup chopped green peppers

½ cup diced tomatoes

1 cup shredded cheese

6 refrigerator biscuits, cut into halves

1. Combine all ingredients except biscuits in slow cooker.

2. Cook on Low for 2 hours.

3. Top with biscuit halves so entire top is covered.

4. Cook for 2 hours longer.

Tropical Pork with Yams

Hope Comerford
Clinton Township, MI

Makes 6 servings
Prep. Time: 15 minutes ⚓ *Cooking Time: 7–8 hours* ⚓ *Ideal slow-cooker size: 5-qt.*

2–3-lb. pork loin

Salt, to taste

Pepper, to taste

1 (20-oz.) can crushed pineapple

¼ cup honey

¼ cup brown sugar

¼ cup apple cider vinegar

1 tsp. low-sodium soy sauce

4 yams, cut into bite-sized chunks

1. Spray the crock with nonstick spray.

2. Lay the pork loin at the bottom of the crock and sprinkle it with salt and pepper on both sides.

3. In a separate bowl, combine the pineapple, honey, brown sugar, apple cider vinegar, and soy sauce. Mix together.

4. Place the chunks of yams over and around the pork loin and then pour the pineapple sauce over the top.

5. Cover and cook on Low for 7 to 8 hours.

Vegetarian and Seafood One-Pot Meals

Crustless Spinach Quiche

Barbara Hoover
Landisville, PA

Makes 8 servings

Prep. Time: 15 minutes ⚜ Cooking Time: 2–4 hours ⚜ Ideal slow-cooker size: 3- or 4-qt.

2 (10-oz.) pkgs. frozen chopped spinach

2 cups cottage cheese

4 Tbsp. (½ stick) butter, cut into pieces

1½ cups sharp cheese, cubed

3 eggs, beaten

¼ cup flour

1 tsp. salt

1. Grease interior of slow-cooker crock.

2. Thaw spinach completely. Squeeze as dry as you can. Then place in crock.

3. Stir in all other ingredients and combine well.

4. Cover. Cook on Low for 2 to 4 hours, or until quiche is set. Stick blade of knife into center of quiche. If blade comes out clean, quiche is set. If it doesn't, cover and cook another 15 minutes or so.

5. When cooked, allow to stand for 10 to 15 minutes so mixture can firm up. Then serve.

Variations:

1. Double the recipe if you wish. Cook it in a 5-qt. slow cooker.

2. Omit cottage cheese. Add 1 cup milk, 1 tsp. baking powder, and increase flour to 1 cup instead.

3. Reserve sharp cheese and sprinkle on top. Allow to melt before serving.

—Barbara Jean Fabel

Mexican Breakfast Casserole

Hope Comerford
Clinton Township, MI

Makes 4 servings
Prep. Time: 20 minutes ♣ *Cooking Time: 7–8 hours* ♣ *Ideal slow-cooker size: 3-qt.*

8 eggs

1½ cups milk

1 tsp. salt

1 tsp. pepper

¾ cup picante sauce (such as Pace Mild)—this equals about half a jar

1 small onion, chopped

½ jalapeño pepper, seeds removed, minced

1 cup frozen corn

2 cups shredded Mexican blend cheese, *divided*

9 (or more) white corn tortillas (5¾-inch recommended)

7 oz. (or so) chorizo, removed from the casing, divided

1. Mix together the eggs, milk, salt, pepper, picante sauce, onion, jalapeño, corn, and 1 cup shredded Mexican blend cheese.

2. Spray your crock with nonstick spray.

3. Line the bottom of the crock with approximately 3 white corn tortillas.

4. Pour half of the egg mixture over this and then crumble half of the chorizo on top. Repeat this process with another layer of tortillas, egg mixture, and the remaining chorizo.

5. Top with a final layer of tortillas and the remaining cheese on top.

6. Cover and cook on Low for 7 to 8 hours.

Zucchini Casserole

Mary Clair Wenger
Kimmswick, MO

Makes 8 servings
Prep. Time: 25 minutes ♣ *Cooking Time: 4–5 hours* ♣ *Ideal slow-cooker size: 4-qt.*

5 cups diced zucchini
1 cup grated carrots
1 small onion, diced finely
1½ cups biscuit baking mix
½ cup grated Parmesan cheese
4 eggs, beaten
¼ cup olive oil
2 tsp. dried marjoram
½ tsp. salt
Pepper, to taste

1. Mix together all ingredients. Pour into greased slow cooker.

2. Cover and cook on Low for 4 to 5 hours, until set. Remove lid last 30 minutes to allow excess moisture to evaporate.

3. Serve hot or at room temperature.

Zucchini-Vegetable Pot

Edwina Stoltzfus
Narvon, PA

Makes 6 servings

Prep. Time: 40 minutes ♣ *Cooking Time: 3–4 hours* ♣ *Ideal slow-cooker size: 3½- or 4-qt.*

2 cups diced zucchini

2 stalks celery, chopped

¼ cup chopped green bell peppers

I large onion, chopped

2 large tomatoes, chopped

¼ cup brown rice, uncooked

¾ tsp. sea salt

¼ tsp. garlic powder

⅛ tsp. nutmeg

¼ tsp. black pepper

I tsp. gluten-free Worcestershire sauce

1. Place vegetables in slow cooker. Top with rice and sprinkle with seasonings.

2. Cover and cook on High for 3 to 4 hours.

Double Corn Tortilla Bake

Kathy Keener Shantz, Lancaster, PA

Makes 4 servings

Prep. Time: 15 minutes ⚖ *Cooking Time: 2–3 hours* ⚖ *Ideal slow-cooker size: 3- or 4-qt.*

8 corn tortillas, *divided*

1½ cups shredded Monterey Jack cheese, *divided*

1 cup corn, fresh, frozen, or canned (drained of water), *divided*

4 green onions, sliced, about ½ cup, *divided*

2 eggs, beaten

1 cup buttermilk

1 (4-oz.) can diced green chilies

1. Grease interior of slow-cooker crock.

2. Tear 4 tortillas into bite-sized pieces. Scatter evenly over bottom of crock.

3. Top with half the cheese, half the corn, and half the green onions.

4. Repeat layers.

5. In a mixing bowl, stir together eggs, buttermilk, and chilies. Gently pour over tortilla mixture.

6. Cover. Cook on Low for 2 to 3 hours, or until knife inserted in center comes out clean.

Rice, Corn, and Cheese Casserole

Sara Harter Fredette
Williamsburg, MA

Makes 6–8 servings
Prep. Time: 10 minutes 🎋 *Cooking Time: 3–4 hours* 🎋 *Ideal slow-cooker size: 4-qt.*

3 cups cooked rice

I (15-oz.) can whole-kernel corn, drained

I small onion, chopped

2 cups grated sharp cheddar cheese

I½ cups milk

½ tsp. salt

½ tsp. chili powder

¼ tsp. pepper

1. Grease interior of slow-cooker crock.

2. Add all ingredients and stir to mix.

3. Cook on Low for 3 to 4 hours or until set.

Vegetables and Red Quinoa Casserole

Gladys Voth
Hesston, KS

Makes 6–8 servings

Prep. Time: 20 minutes & Cooking Time: 1½–4 hours & Ideal slow-cooker size: 4-qt.

4 cups peeled and cubed butternut squash

2 cups peeled and cubed beets (¾-inch in size)

2 cups sliced celery (½-inch thick), about 2 stalks

6 cloves garlic

1½ cups vegetable broth

3 Tbsp. dried basil

1 cup uncooked red quinoa, rinsed and drained

Mixed-berry almond nondairy yogurt, for topping

½ cup cashew nuts, for topping

1. Grease interior of slow-cooker crock.

2. Place butternut squash, beets, and celery in crock.

3. Coarsely chop garlic cloves. Place in crock.

4. Pour vegetable broth over ingredients in slow cooker.

5. Crush dried basil between fingers while adding to slow cooker.

6. Stir everything together well.

7. Cover. Cook on High for 1½ to 2 hours or on Low for 3 to 4 hours.

8. About 30 minutes before end of cooking time, stir in quinoa. Cover and cook on High for 20 to 30 minutes.

9. Serve hot or at room temperature.

10. Top each serving with nondairy yogurt and a sprinkling of cashews.

Thai Veggie Curry

Christen Chew
Lancaster, PA

Makes 4–5 servings

Prep. Time: 30 minutes ⚮ *Cooking Time: 5–6 hours* ⚮ *Ideal slow-cooker size: 4- or 5-qt.*

2 large carrots, thinly sliced

1 medium onion, chopped

3 cloves garlic, chopped

2 large potatoes, peeled or not, diced

1 (15½-oz.) can garbanzo beans, rinsed and drained

1 (14½-oz.) can diced tomatoes, undrained

2 Tbsp. curry powder

1 tsp. ground coriander

1 tsp. cayenne pepper

2 cups vegetable stock

½ cup frozen green peas

½ cup coconut milk

Salt, to taste

1. Grease interior of slow-cooker crock.

2. Stir all ingredients except peas, coconut milk, and salt into crock. Mix together well, making sure seasonings are distributed throughout.

3. Cover. Cook on Low for 5 to 6 hours, or until vegetables are as tender as you like them.

4. Just before serving, stir in peas and coconut milk. Season with salt to taste.

Doris's Broccoli and Cauliflower with Cheese

Doris G. Herr
Manheim, PA

Makes 4–6 servings
Prep. Time: 5 minutes   &   Cooking Time: 1½–3 hours   &   Ideal slow-cooker size: 3-qt.

1 lb. frozen cauliflower, chopped

2 (10-oz.) pkgs. frozen broccoli, chopped

½ cup water

2 cups shredded cheddar cheese

1. Place cauliflower and broccoli in slow cooker.

2. Add water. Top with cheese.

3. Cook on Low for 1½ to 3 hours, depending on how crunchy or soft you want the vegetables.

Herbed Rice and Lentil Bake

Peg Zannotti
Tulsa, OK

Makes 4 servings
Prep. Time: 15 minutes ❧ *Cooking Time: 2–4 hours* ❧ *Ideal slow-cooker size: 4-qt.*

2⅔ cups vegetable broth or water

¾ cup dried green lentils, picked over for any stones and rinsed

¾ cup chopped onions

½ cup uncooked brown rice

¼ cup dry white wine or water

½ tsp. dried basil

¼ tsp. dried oregano

¼ tsp. dried thyme

⅛ tsp. garlic powder

½ cup shredded Italian-mix cheese or cheddar cheese

1. Grease interior of slow-cooker crock.

2. Place everything in the crock, except cheese. Stir together until well mixed.

3. Cover. Cook on Low for 3 to 4 hours, or on High for 2 to 3 hours, or until lentils and rice are both as tender as you like them.

4. Just before serving, sprinkle top with cheese. Allow to melt, and then serve.

Variations:

1. Add ½ tsp. salt in step 2 if you wish.

2. Before adding cheese, top mixture with ½ cup Italian-flavored panko bread crumbs. Cook, uncovered, 5–10 minutes. Sprinkle with cheese. Allow cheese to melt, and then serve.

Jambalaya

Doris M. Coyle-Zipp
South Ozone Park, NY

Makes 5–6 servings
Prep. Time: 15 minutes ⚜ *Cooking Time: 2¼–3¾ hours* ⚜ *Ideal slow-cooker size: 5-qt.*

3½–4-lb. roasting chicken, cut up

3 onions, diced

1 carrot, sliced

3–4 cloves garlic, minced

1 tsp. dried oregano

1 tsp. dried basil

1 tsp. salt

⅛ tsp. white pepper

1 (14-oz.) can crushed tomatoes

1 lb. shelled raw shrimp

2 cups cooked rice

1. Combine all ingredients except shrimp and rice in slow cooker.

2. Cover. Cook on Low for 2 to 3½ hours, or until chicken is tender.

3. Add shrimp and rice.

4. Cover. Cook on High for 15 to 20 minutes, or until shrimp are done.

One-Pot Pasta Meals

Hot Tuna Macaroni Casserole

Dorothy VanDeest
Memphis, TN

Makes 6 servings
Prep. Time: 15 minutes   ❧   Cooking Time: 2–6 hours   ❧   Ideal slow-cooker size: 3-qt.

2 (6-oz.) cans tuna, water-packed, rinsed and drained

1½ cups cooked macaroni

½ cup finely chopped onions

¼ cup finely chopped green bell peppers

1 (4-oz.) can sliced mushrooms, drained

1 (10-oz.) pkg. frozen cauliflower, partially thawed

½ cup low-sodium, fat-free chicken broth

1. Combine all ingredients in slow cooker. Stir well.

2. Cover. Cook on Low for 4 to 6 hours or on High for 2 to 3 hours.

Mexi Chicken Rotini

Jane Geigley, Lancaster, PA

Makes 6 servings
Prep. Time: 30 minutes ❧ *Cooking Time: 4½ hours* ❧ *Ideal slow-cooker size: 4-qt.*

1 cup water

3 cups partially cooked rotini

1 (12-oz.) pkg. frozen mixed vegetables

1 (10-oz.) can Ro*Tel diced tomatoes with green chilies

1 (4-oz.) can green chilies, undrained

4 cups shredded cooked chicken

1 cup low-fat shredded cheddar cheese

1. Combine all ingredients in slow cooker except shredded cheddar.

2. Cover and cook on Low for 4 hours.

3. Top with shredded cheddar, then let cook covered an additional 20 minutes or so, or until cheese is melted.

Baked Ziti

Hope Comerford, Clinton Township, MI

Makes 8 servings
Prep. Time: 15 minutes   &   Cooking Time: 4 hours   &   Ideal slow-cooker size: 5-qt.

1 (28-oz.) can low-sodium crushed tomatoes

1 (15-oz.) can low-sodium tomato sauce

1½ tsp. Italian seasoning

1 tsp. garlic powder

1 tsp. onion powder

1 tsp. pepper

1 tsp. sea salt

1 lb. ziti or rigatoni pasta, uncooked, *divided*

1–2 cups low-fat shredded mozzarella cheese, *divided*

1. Spray crock with nonstick spray.

2. In a bowl, mix together crushed tomatoes, tomato sauce, Italian seasoning, garlic powder, onion powder, pepper, and salt.

3. In the bottom of the crock, pour ⅓ of the pasta sauce.

4. Add ½ of the pasta on top of the sauce.

5. Add another ⅓ of your pasta sauce.

6. Spread ½ of the mozzarella cheese on top of that.

7. Add the remaining pasta, the remaining sauce, and the remaining cheese on top of that.

8. Cover and cook on Low for 4 hours.

Fresh Veggie Lasagna

Deanne Gingrich, Lancaster, PA

Makes 4–6 servings
Prep. Time: 30 minutes ✿ *Cooking Time: 4 hours* ✿ *Ideal slow-cooker size: 4- or 5-qt.*

1½ cups shredded low-fat mozzarella cheese

½ cup low-fat ricotta cheese

⅓ cup grated Parmesan cheese

1 egg, lightly beaten

1 tsp. dried oregano

¼ tsp. garlic powder

3 cups marinara sauce, *divided*

1 medium zucchini, diced, *divided*

4 uncooked lasagna noodles

4 cups fresh baby spinach, *divided*

1 cup sliced fresh mushrooms, *divided*

1. Grease interior of slow-cooker crock.

2. In a bowl, mix together mozzarella, ricotta, and Parmesan cheeses, egg, oregano, and garlic powder. Set aside.

3. Spread ½ cup marinara sauce in crock.

4. Sprinkle with half the zucchini.

5. Spoon ⅓ of cheese mixture over zucchini.

6. Break 2 noodles into large pieces to cover cheese layer.

7. Spread ½ cup marinara over the noodles.

8. Top with half the spinach and then half the mushrooms.

9. Repeat layers, ending with cheese mixture, and then sauce. Press layers down firmly.

10. Cover and cook on Low for 4 hours, or until vegetables are as tender as you like them and noodles are fully cooked.

11. Let stand 15 minutes so lasagna can firm up before serving.

Tortellini with Broccoli

Susan Kasting
Jenks, OK

Makes 4 servings
Prep. Time: 10 minutes ⚘ *Cooking Time: 2½–3 hours* ⚘ *Ideal slow-cooker size: 4-qt.*

½ cup water

1 (26-oz.) jar pasta sauce, your favorite

1 Tbsp. Italian seasoning

1 (9-oz.) pkg. frozen spinach and cheese tortellini

1 (16-oz.) pkg. frozen broccoli florets

1. In a bowl, mix water, pasta sauce, and seasoning together.

2. Pour ⅓ of sauce into bottom of slow cooker. Top with all the tortellini.

3. Pour ⅓ of sauce over tortellini. Top with broccoli.

4. Pour remaining sauce over broccoli.

5. Cook on High for 2½ to 3 hours, or until broccoli and pasta are tender but not mushy.

Slow-Cooker Mac and Cheese

Jessica Stoner, Plain City, OH

Makes 4–6 servings

Prep. Time: 15–20 minutes   *Cooking Time: 3½ hours*   *Ideal slow-cooker size: 3-qt.*

4 cups cooked gluten-free elbow macaroni (1 cup dry)

2 eggs, beaten

1 cup low-fat shredded mild cheddar cheese

2 cups low-fat shredded sharp cheddar cheese

1 (12-oz.) can low-fat or fat-free evaporated milk

½ cup fat-free milk

2 Tbsp. butter, melted, *optional*

1 tsp. sea salt

Pinch pepper

1. Place cooked macaroni in slow cooker.

2. Mix all other ingredients in a separate bowl.

3. Pour over macaroni. Don't stir!

4. Cover and cook on Low for 3½ hours.

Metric Equivalent Measurements

If you're accustomed to using metric measurements, I don't want you to be inconvenienced by the imperial measurements I use in this book.

Use this handy chart, too, to figure out the size of the slow cooker you'll need for each recipe.

Weight (Dry Ingredients)

1 oz		30 g
4 oz	¼ lb	120 g
8 oz	½ lb	240 g
12 oz	¾ lb	360 g
16 oz	1 lb	480 g
32 oz	2 lb	960 g

Slow Cooker Sizes

1-quart	0.96 l
2-quart	1.92 l
3-quart	2.88 l
4-quart	3.84 l
5-quart	4.80 l
6-quart	5.76 l
7-quart	6.72 l
8-quart	7.68 l

Volume (Liquid Ingredients)

½ tsp.		2 ml
1 tsp.		5 ml
1 Tbsp.	½ fl oz	15 ml
2 Tbsp.	1 fl oz	30 ml
¼ cup	2 fl oz	60 ml
⅓ cup	3 fl oz	80 ml
½ cup	4 fl oz	120 ml
⅔ cup	5 fl oz	160 ml
¾ cup	6 fl oz	180 ml
1 cup	8 fl oz	240 ml
1 pt	16 fl oz	480 ml
1 qt	32 fl oz	960 ml

Length

¼ in	6 mm
½ in	13 mm
¾ in	19 mm
1 in	25 mm
6 in	15 cm
12 in	30 cm

Recipe and Ingredient Index

About the Author

Hope Comerford is a mom, wife, elementary music teacher, blogger, recipe developer, public speaker, ALM Zone fit leader, Young Living Essential Oils essential oil enthusiast/educator, and published author.

Growing up, Hope spent many hours in the kitchen with her Meme (grandmother), and her love for cooking grew from there. While working on her master's degree when her daughter was young, Hope turned to her slow cookers for some salvation and sanity. It was from there she began truly experimenting with recipes and quickly learned she had the ability to get a little more creative in the kitchen and develop her own recipes.

In 2010, Hope started her blog, *A Busy Mom's Slow Cooker Adventures*, to simply share the recipes she was making with her family and friends. She never imagined people all over the world would begin visiting her page and sharing her recipes with others as well. In 2013, Hope self-published her first cookbook, *Slow Cooker Recipes: 10 Ingredients or Less and Gluten-Free*, and then later wrote *The Gluten-Free Slow Cooker*.

Hope became the new brand ambassador and author of Fix-It and Forget-It in mid-2016. Since then, she has brought her excitement and creativity to the Fix-It and Forget-It brand.

Hope lives in the city of Clinton Township, Michigan, near Metro Detroit. She's been a native of Michigan her whole life. She has been happily married to her husband and best friend, Justin, since 2008. Together they have two children, Ella and Gavin, who are her motivation, inspiration, and heart. In her spare time, Hope enjoys traveling, singing, cooking, reading books, spending time with friends and family, and relaxing.

FIX-IT and FORGET-IT®
NEW COOKBOOK

250 new delicious slow cooker recipes!

Phyllis Good

New York Times bestselling author **Phyllis Good**

FIX-IT and FORGET-IT®
BAKING
with your
SLOW COOKER

150 Slow Cooker Recipes for Breads, Pizza, Cakes, Tarts, Crisps, Bars, Pies, Cupcakes, and More!

FIX-IT and FORGET-IT®
Lazy AND Slow COOKBOOK

365 Days of SLOW COOKER Recipes

HOPE COMERFORD

NEW YORK TIMES BESTSELLING SERIES

FIX-IT and FORGET-IT®
Healthy
SLOW COOKER COOKBOOK

New York Times Bestselling Series

150 Whole Food Recipes for Paleo, Vegan, Gluten-Free, and Diabetic-Friendly Diets

HOPE COMERFORD

NEW YORK TIMES BESTSELLING SERIES

FIX-IT and FORGET-IT®
FAVORITE SLOW COOKER RECIPES FOR MOM

150 recipes mom will love to make, eat, and share!

HOPE COMERFORD

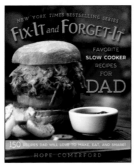

NEW YORK TIMES BESTSELLING SERIES

FIX-IT and FORGET-IT®
FAVORITE SLOW COOKER RECIPES FOR DAD

150 recipes dad will love to make, eat, and share!

HOPE COMERFORD

FIX-IT and FORGET-IT®
SLOW COOKER Champion Recipes

450 OF OUR VERY BEST RECIPES

PHYLLIS GOOD

By the New York Times bestselling author

FIX-IT and FORGET-IT®

A $47.85 VALUE!

BOX SET

PHYLLIS GOOD

FIX-IT and FORGET-IT®
INSTANT POT COOKBOOK

100 DELICIOUS INSTANT POT RECIPES!

HOPE COMERFORD

NEW YORK TIMES BESTSELLING SERIES

FIX-IT and FORGET-IT®
INSTANT POT DIABETES COOKBOOK

HOPE COMERFORD

127 SUPER EASY HEALING RECIPES

FIX-IT and FORGET-IT®
SLOW COOKER FREEZER MEALS

150 MAKE-AHEAD MEALS TO SAVE YOU TIME AND MONEY

NEW YORK TIMES BESTSELLING SERIES

NEW YORK TIMES BESTSELLING SERIES

FIX-IT and FORGET-IT®
COOKING FOR TWO

150 SMALL-BATCH SLOW COOKER RECIPES

HOPE COMERFORD

NEW YORK TIMES BESTSELLING SERIES

FIX-IT and FORGET-IT®
BEST SLOW COOKER CHICKEN RECIPES

QUICK AND EASY DINNERS, CASSEROLES, SOUPS & STEWS, AND MORE!

150 DELICIOUS RECIPES

HOPE COMERFORD

#1 *New York Times* bestseller!

FIX-IT and FORGET-IT®
Cookbook
REVISED & UPDATED

700 Great Slow Cooker Recipes

Phyllis Pellman Good

FIX-IT and FORGET-IT®
kids' Cookbook

50 Favorite Recipes to Make in a Slow Cooker
Phyllis Pellman Good

By The *New York Times* bestselling author

FIX-IT and FORGET-IT®
BIG COOKBOOK

1400 Best Slow Cooker Recipes!

Phyllis Pellman Good